IN A
HOTEL

DEBORAH FOX

EVANS BROTHERS LIMITED

Published by Evans Brothers Limited
2a Portman Mansions
Chiltern Street
London
W1M 1LE

© 2000 Evans Brothers Limited

First published in 2000

All rights reserved. No part of this publication may be reproduced, stored in a retrieval system or transmitted in any form or by any means, electronic, mechanical, photocopying, recording or otherwise, without prior permission of Evans Brothers Limited.

Commissioned by: Su Swallow
Design: Neil Sayer
Photography: Gareth Boden and Alan Towse
Illustrator: Liam Bonney/The Art Market

British Library Cataloguing in Publication Data

Fox, Deborah
 People at work in a hotel
 1.Hotels - Juvenile literature 2. Hotels - Employees - Juvenile literature
 I.Title II.In a hotel
 647.6'4

ISBN 023751964X

Printed in Hong Kong by Wing King Tong

Acknowledgements

The author and publisher wish to thank the following for their help and co-operation:
Hannah Smith of Marriotts, Gary Moran, Tony Owen, Zelica Carr, Simon Johnson, Mark Astbury and all the staff at the Mariott Breadsall Priory, Derby. Thanks also to Sue Barr and the staff at Marriott Manchester.

All photographs by Gareth Boden except for the following by Alan Towse: p. 18 (bottom left and right), 21, 22 (bottom) and 23 (left and top).

Contents

Checking in	8
Making sales	10
Cleaning the hotel	12
Conferences and weddings	14
Looking after the hotel	16
In the kitchen	18
In the restaurant	20
Learning on the job	22
Sport and leisure	24
At the end of a day	26
Glossary	28
Index	29

Checking in

I'm Tony and I'm an Operations Manager at a large hotel. Each department in the hotel has a manager. If any of the managers looking after reception, maintenance, conferences, cleaning and the restaurant have any problems, they come to me. I have to make sure all these departments work well and keep to their spending budgets.

Morning meetings

Every morning, except at the weekend, there is a short meeting in the General Manager's office with one person from each department. We discuss any special events going on that day, whether any important visitors like football or tennis players are arriving, and how many people are booked in for the night.

Booking a room

There are 112 rooms at this hotel and about 230 members of staff. Our busiest months are from June to September. People who want to book a room telephone one of our reservations agents. All the information the agent needs is displayed on the computer screen – the price of the rooms and which ones are free. One agent answers about 130 calls a day and most of these calls are made at lunchtime. We have extra staff working at peak times.

▲ Staff from all departments come to the morning meeting to find out what is happening that day.

◀ The reservations agent wears headphones so that she can listen to the caller and type in information at the same time.

▲ The concierge helps the guests with their luggage.

Checking in

All new guests go to the reception desk, where the hotel receptionists check their booking and hand over the room keys. We have two concierges at this hotel who help guests with their luggage. The concierges know a lot about the local area and can give advice to guests on places worth visiting. This area of the hotel is known as 'front of house' and a manager looks after the twelve staff who work here.

I went to catering college when I left school because I wanted to be a chef. I've worked in London as a trainee chef, on a cruise ship as a waiter and then I became a Food and Beverages Manager. I've had to move around a lot to get this job, and long hours are normal. I've had one day off in the last three weeks. But I love the atmosphere in hotels, meeting lots of new people and the fact that every day brings something new.

Making sales

We want lots of people to stay here ... the busier, the better! Companies hold conferences at the hotel, people have weddings here, we have golf tournaments and there is a leisure club and a gym. In our sales office two people look after conference bookings, one person deals with golf bookings, another is responsible for weddings and Christmas bookings and one sends out brochures. The Revenue Manager is the head of the team.

Sales meetings

To keep up to date with how bookings are going, there are regular sales meetings. The General Manager runs the hotel and he is keen to discuss how we can increase business in the next few months. The financial

▲ The sales team look after wedding, conference and golf bookings.

▶ Nicky deals with conference bookings. She discusses an enquiry with Matthew from the conference team.

10

▲ The General Manager (second from the left) discusses ideas for bringing in new business with other managers.

controller hands out the figures showing how busy the hotel is and how much money the leisure facilities, golf, conferences and weddings are bringing in. The area sales manager is our link with local businesses. She visits new people to tell them about the hotel.

> I have targets to meet – to sell so many rooms a year. I know our busiest and our quietest times. I need to think of ways to boost sales in our quieter months and I must make sure we are one step ahead of our competitors.
>
> Clare, Revenue Manager

▲ The area sales manager is 'out on the road' most of the time.

11

Cleaning the hotel

The hotel and the bedrooms have to be cleaned every day. The department responsible for cleaning is called 'housekeeping'. We have a head housekeeper who manages 30 members of staff. Quite a few of them work part-time. Each room attendant has from six to thirteen rooms to clean each day, depending on the size of the room. They clean the bathrooms, change the towels and toiletries, make beds, clean and polish the furniture and re-stock the tea, coffee and biscuits.

> I always do things in the same order, because it's quicker if you have a system. I make the beds first and then I polish and tidy. I make sure the notepads and leaflets are there. Then I move on to the bathroom. If we have any important guests staying, we put champagne, fruit baskets and mineral water in the room, and, at night, we come back to turn down the bed, draw the curtains, turn on the light and leave a sweet on the pillow.
>
> Val, room attendant

◀ All the room attendants are trained on the job. They learn, for example, how to turn down the sheets in a certain way. A supervisor checks their rooms until they are fully trained.

▶ The room attendant, Carol, checks that her trolley is well stocked with sheets, pillowcases, shampoos, soap, tea, coffee and biscuits before she starts cleaning her rooms.

Head housekeeper

Our head housekeeper has to order all the supplies, from cleaning fluids to shampoos and soaps. She must keep to her spending budget. She also hires staff and organises their training and hours, she talks to other hotels in our group to compare costs, and she arranges for our towels and linen to be cleaned by outside businesses.

▼ All the used sheets and towels need to be sorted into piles by one of the linen porters. Then outside cleaners pick them up and return them the next day.

Costs of cleaning
- Each room attendant has about 25 minutes to clean each room.
- Cleaning fluids cost about 20p per room, but coffee, tea, biscuits, shampoo and soap cost about £1.80 per room.
- In one busy month we use about 6000 sheets and 6000 towels.

Conferences and weddings

> This year I've taken bookings for over 90 weddings and I've helped with arrangements on all of them, such as hiring a photographer and suggesting florists. I can spend over a year planning a wedding with a couple. It's fantastic to see everything come together on the day.
>
> Nicola, wedding coordinator

We have two weddings at the hotel today. Our wedding coordinator wants to make sure everything is going according to plan. The florist has been decorating the rooms with flowers and the banqueting staff have set the tables.

▲ I have a quick chat with Nicola, our wedding coordinator. Everything is on time and there are no problems.

◀ The banqueting staff polish the glasses for one of our wedding receptions.

▲ One of the supervisors prepares a conference room. He sorts out folders and pens and makes sure the overhead projector is working.

Conferences

We have up to nine rooms available for conferences and if they are all being used we could have 300 people here on the same day! Conferences have to be well organised. People want tea and coffee breaks, lunch and sometimes dinner. Some conferences may last a few days and so the visitors need rooms too. We have a conference manager who is in charge of a team of six.

I come in at 6.30am. I check the rooms that have been set up the night before. When the conference delegates arrive, I introduce myself. I give them a walkie-talkie and explain how it works! They can then contact me at any time during the day.
I enjoy the fact that I'm not stuck in a stuffy office all day. The hours are long in hotels, but there's a lot of freedom in my job.

Neil, conference team

Looking after the hotel

There are two 18-hole golf courses here. To keep them in tip-top condition we have a team of ten groundstaff. Every day they rake the bunkers, roll the putting greens to keep them nice and flat and mow the grass. They work outside all the time, whether it's sunny or snowing. We also have a gardener who looks after the gardens all year – 2 hectares in total.

▼ The bunkers on the golf courses have to be raked every day.

▲ The greenkeepers cut out new holes on the putting greens and fill in the old ones. This keeps the greens in good condition and makes the course more interesting for the regular golfers.

◀ One new hole in the putting green.

The maintenance department

There are always little problems to sort out around the hotel. A tap may be leaking, a drain might be blocked, doors come loose and lightbulbs have to be changed. The Property Manager is in charge of a department that sorts out these day-to-day problems. He also organises new building projects. There are three people in the maintenance department – two engineers and a decorator. If the room attendants find any problems when they are cleaning, they fill out job request cards and hand them to maintenance.

▼ One of the engineers checks the water-filtering system for the swimming pool.

> We need to build a new staff canteen at the hotel. I enjoy getting my teeth into a big job like that – sorting out the costs, the plans, the outside builders and the schedule.
>
> Gordon, Property Manager

▲ The decorator does some work in one of the bathrooms.

How much?

- The hotel spends about £350 a month on lightbulbs.
- The electricity bill is about £7000 a month in summer and £10,500 in winter.
- We spend nearly £29,000 a year on water. We use a lot of water sprinkling the putting greens.

17

In the kitchen

The kitchen is busy from 5 o'clock in the morning, when the breakfast chef starts preparing breakfasts, until midnight, when the chefs have finished cooking dinner. The head chef is in charge of 32 staff. There is a team of chefs who work in the different sections of the kitchen – pastry chefs, sauce chefs, vegetable chefs and larder chefs, who prepare salads.

▲ Every day the head chef has a meeting with other chefs to discuss what they will be doing that day.

▽ A chef checks the milk delivery.

Deliveries

Fresh vegetables, milk, bread, meat and fish are delivered to the kitchens every day. The food has to be date-

▷ A chef runs through an order in the dairy store-room.

18

stamped and stored at the correct temperature. We have huge walk-in refridgerators and freezers, chiller rooms for food that needs to be kept cool, and dry store-rooms for tins, bottles and packets.

Preparing food

Our head chef plans all the menus with his deputy, the sous chef, a week in advance. Some things can be prepared ahead of time, like pastries and desserts, sauces, pies and cold meats. Then the chefs have more time to cook the fresh food.

▶ The senior pastry chef decorates some desserts she and her junior chef prepared earlier. They are kept in one of our dairy fridges until they are served.

◀ The desserts keep cool in one of our dairy fridges.

Food facts
- The head chef can spend up to £40,000 a month on food.
- On a very busy day we can have 1000 meals to prepare.
- Every month the head chef orders 500 sausages, 400 eggs and 3360 litres of milk.
- 'Sous' is French for 'under'. The sous chef works for the head chef.

Every day we have 'specials' on the menu, only for that day. Any one of the chefs can make a suggestion and choose the recipe. Whoever gets the most orders has to buy all the other chefs in the kitchen a drink!

Mark, sous chef

In the restaurant

The restaurant is calm and quiet with soft music playing in the background, unlike the kitchen, which is hot, stuffy and very noisy. The head chef or sous chef is shouting out orders and the kitchen staff are rushing around cooking the food, banging dishes and clattering plates.

Tasting panel

We like our waiters and waitresses to taste the food we serve each evening. So, before the restaurant is open, we have a tasting panel, where some of the staff sample a starter, a main course and a dessert. They have to mark each dish out of ten.

▲ All our waiters and waitresses know how to set the tables correctly. They are told how many tables to prepare each evening.

▶ Every evening some of the waiters and waitresses sample the 'special' that is on the menu that night. They give the different courses marks out of ten and pass their comments to the head chef.

20

◀ The sous chef checks that the food is well presented before he allows the waitress to take it away.

Behind the scenes

Every evening either the head chef or the sous chef is on duty and in charge of the kitchen. When an order comes through, the chef in charge shouts "Check on" to the other chefs and then, "Table 48: two rump steaks, two fish, one chicken and one pork." The vegetable chefs start cooking the vegetables and the sauce chef and his team start to prepare the main courses. Everything has to come together at the same time. When the chef in charge shouts "Table 48 ready?", that means he wants all the meals to come to him right away.

We used to have a sign on the kitchen door saying "Smile, you're on stage!" When you're carrying a huge, heavy tray and the kitchen is hot and stuffy, smiling isn't always the first thing on your mind!

I started working here as a part-time waitress six years ago and I worked my way up. Now I look after all the waiting staff and plan their hours and the rotas. My working hours are a bit anti-social. I start at 1 or 2 o'clock in the afternoon most days and finish at midnight.

Andrea, head of restaurant waiting staff

Learning on the job

When new trainee waiters and waitresses arrive at the hotel, they have a short training course and then they are teamed up with more experienced staff for 90 days.

Training for chefs

New chefs need to get experience in all areas of the kitchen (see page 18). The sous chef organises on-the-job training. The most experienced chefs apart from the head and sous chefs, are the sauce chefs. They have gained experience in all sections of the kitchen. As well as

▲ This trainee waiter has been teamed with an experienced waitress. She checks through an order with him to make sure they haven't forgotten anything.

▶ Serving lunch in the main restaurant.

◀ This pastry chef presses hot almond biscuits around a mould.

◀ Making maple-leaf biscuits.

▼ One of the larder chefs slices up a selection of cheeses.

cooking sauces, they prepare the main courses and organise the food for weddings and banquets.

When I started working here two and a half years ago, I made sandwiches in the hotel cafe bar. I've worked my way up to sauce chef. Working for a large hotel group has given me good training and a lot of opportunities.

Simon, sauce chef

Working as a chef is physically demanding. We have to lift heavy pots and pans because we're cooking for so many people and our menu is so vast. The kitchen gets incredibly hot too.

Mark, sous chef

23

Sport and leisure

Our leisure club is busiest at weekends. We have day members who use the swimming pool, sauna, jacuzzi, gym and dance studio, as well as the guests. There are 25 people working here and a leisure manager, and we also employ staff to run a "kids' club" in the school holidays and on some weekends. The leisure staff make sure that the pool area is clean. They check the chlorine level and the temperature of the pool, clear away used towels and get new ones from housekeeping, refill the shampoo and soap dispensers in the changing rooms and they look after the guests when they arrive.

▲ Leisure-club staff check the pool temperature four times a day. It is 31°C, which is just right.

Golf

Our busiest golf months are June and September when companies book golf tournaments for their staff and

All through the year

- If the golf courses are frosty, we have orange balls for the players.
- At Christmas we have a 'turkey and tinsel tee-off' game. The golfers get turkey sandwiches and mulled wine half-way round the course!
- It costs us about £24,000 a year to run the leisure club.

After I left school, I worked as a lifeguard, an attendant in a leisure club and in the army. Then I came back to work in leisure. Every year I hand in a 'wish-list' to the budget meeting – a list of the new gym equipment I want and the new facilities I'd like.

Warren, leisure manager

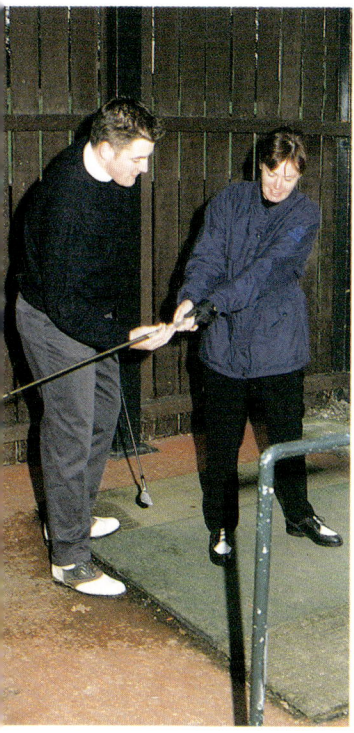

▲ We employ professional golf-players who teach golf. Each lesson is 45 minutes.

guests. The golf manager and her assistant are trying to encourage more guests and companies to play golf all year round. Part of the golf manager's job is to think of new ways to increase the golf bookings for the year.

A course manager looks after the two courses. He checks that the groundstaff are keeping them in tip-top condition. A ranger drives around both golf courses on his buggy every day to make sure that there are no hold-ups or problems on the courses.

Health and beauty salon

There is a team of full-time and part-time beauty therapists here. Some of them are trained in sports massage too. Many guests have driven a long way to get here and may be suffering from back pain.

▶ A part-time beauty therapist uses a heat-treatment lamp for one of the guests who has back pain.

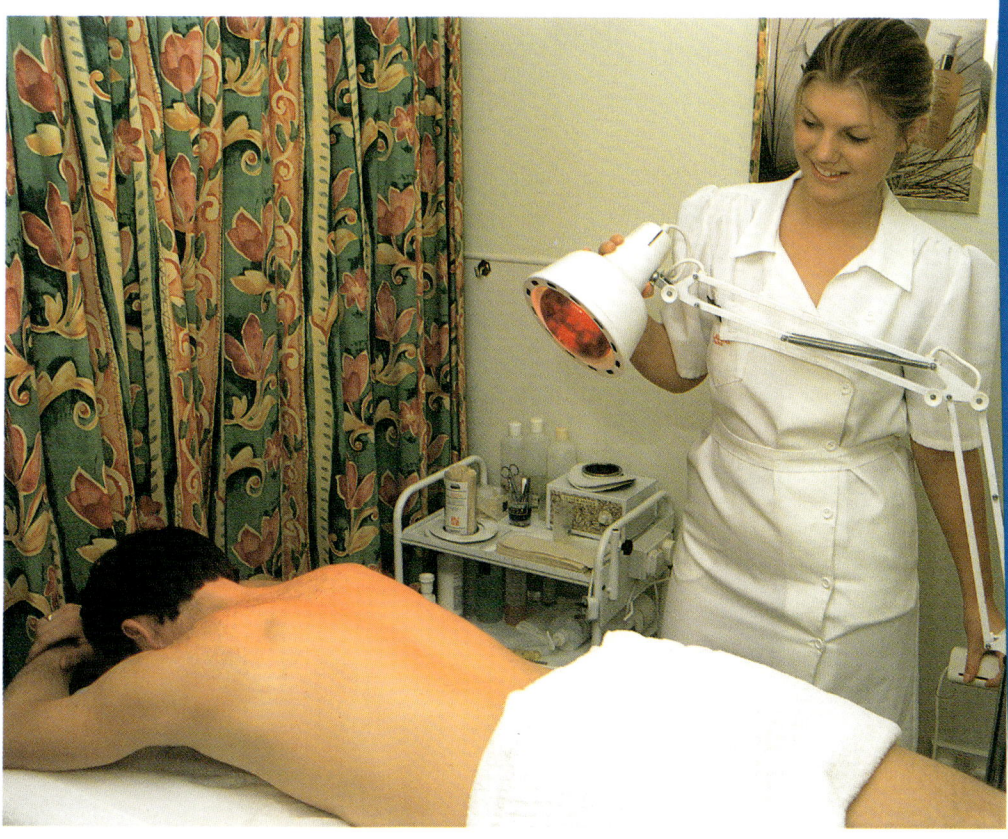

25

At the end of a day

On some days I can work from 11 in the morning until 11 at night, but today I am handing over to the next duty manager at 4pm. The duty manager is in charge for the next shift. If any problems come up, then the duty manager has to sort them out. Last night for instance, we had no hot water and so I spent a few hours with the engineer sorting out the problem. One duty manager always has a brief handover meeting with the next, running through the number of guests staying, whether there have been any problems and how busy the restaurant is. We also walk round the hotel together to check that the fire exits are clear.

▲ The bar manager fills one of the fridges with soft drinks.

Clearing up

The kitchen has to be thoroughly cleaned at the end of each day, ready for the breakfast chef who will arrive at

▶ It's the end of my shift and time to go home. I run through a few points with Janice, the next duty manager.

26

◀ There are large sinks in the kitchens. All the crockery goes into dishwashers, but the large dishes and pans are washed by hand. Washing-up goes on all day, not just at night.

▼ The General Manager and his secretary discuss some letters.

> My office door is always open. When 30,000 guests stay here every year, it's important that the staff work well as a team. They all work hard, are loyal and put in a lot of hours.
>
> Gary, General Manager

5am tomorrow. All the glasses in the bar have to be cleaned and the shelves have to be re-stocked with drinks.

Looking ahead

On Monday I will be having a meeting with the General Manager on the questionnaires we ask our guests to fill in, which show how happy they are with the service, the facilities and the food. We hold regular meetings to check if we can improve on anything. After that I will be having a meeting with the financial controller on the monthly food and housekeeping budgets.

Glossary

area sales manager the person who visits local businesses in order to tell them about the hotel

budget the total amount of money given to a department to spend

bunker a hole filled with sand on a golf course; it acts as an obstacle

"Check on" the sous or head chef shouts out this phrase to the other chefs in the kitchen to let them know he is about to give them the food order

chlorine a disinfectant, or bleach, that kills germs

conference delegates people attending a conference

duty manager the person in charge of the day-to-day running of the hotel for a specific period of time during the day

financial controller the person who manages the money coming in and going out of the hotel

groundstaff the people employed to look after the grounds of the hotel

job request card a card filled in by a room attendant and given to the maintenance department; the card gives details of any jobs that need doing in the rooms or in the hotel, such as a broken cupboard door or a broken lamp

maintenance department the department that looks after the hotel buildings both inside and out

questionnaire a form that asks questions; the reader fills in the answers

ranger the person who inspects the golf courses

revenue the income or amount of money received

'special' part of a meal, usually a main course, which is on the menu just for that day

sous chef the deputy to the head chef

tasting panel three or four waitresses and waiters who taste the 'specials' on the menu and give the food marks out of ten

walkie-talkie a small radio transmitter and receiver, which means the operator can send and receive messages

Index

area sales manager 11, 28

banqueting staff 14
bathrooms 12
beauty therapists 25
breakfast 18, 26
budgets 8, 13, 27, 28

catering 9
chef 9, 18-19, 20-21, 22-23, 26, 28
Christmas 10, 24
cleaning 8, 12-13, 17, 24
concierge 9
conferences 8, 10, 11, 15, 28

decorator 17
deliveries 18
desserts 19, 20
dinner 18
dishwashers 27
duty manager 26, 28

electricity costs 17
engineers 17, 26

financial controller 10-11, 28
fire exits 26
food costs 19, 27

food storage 19

gardens 16
General Manager 8, 10, 27
golf 10, 11, 16, 24-25, 28
greenkeepers 16
groundstaff 16, 24, 28
guest questionnaire 27, 28
gym 10, 24

head chef 18, 19, 20, 21, 22, 28
head housekeeper 12, 13, 27
housekeeping 12, 24, 27

kids' club 24
kitchen 18-19, 21, 22, 23, 26, 27, 28

larder chef 18, 23
leisure club 10, 24

maintenance 8, 17, 28

Operations Manager 8, 14, 26

pastry chef 18, 19

Property Manager 17

reception 8, 9
reservations agents 8, 9
restaurant 8, 20-21, 26
room attendants 12, 13, 17, 28

sauce chef 18, 21, 22, 23
sous chef 19, 20, 21, 22, 28
sports massage 25
swimming pool 17, 24

tasting food 20
training 13, 22

vegetable chef 18, 21

waiter 9, 20, 22, 28
waitresses 20, 21, 22, 28
washing-up 27
water costs 17
weddings 10, 11, 14, 23